FROM BAUHAUS
TO BIRDHOUSE

FROM BAUHAUS TO BIRDHOUSE

LESLIE GARISTO

HarperCollins*Publishers*

FROM BAUHAUS TO BIRDHOUSE was conceived and produced by
Running Heads Incorporated
55 West 21 Street
New York, NY 10010

FIRST EDITION

Editor: Rose K. Phillips
Designer: Julie Duquet
Managing Editor: Jill Hamilton
Production Manager: Peter J. McCulloch
Birdhouse blueprints by Dolores R. Santoliquido

Library of Congress Cataloging-in-Publication Data
Garisto, Leslie
    From bauhaus to birdhouse : imaginative housing for the feathered
community / by Leslie Garisto. — 1st ed.
        p.   cm.
Includes bibliographical references and index.
ISBN 0-06-016742-4 (cloth) : $20.00
1. Birdhouses.   2. Birds, Attracting of.   I. Title.
QL676.5.G37   1992
598'.07234—dc20   91-50484
                                                         CIP

Typeset by Trufont Typographers, Inc.
Color separations by Hong Kong Scanner Craft Co., Ltd.
Printed and bound in Singapore by Tieh Wah Press (Pte.) Ltd.

92 93 94 95 96 10 9 8 7 6 4 3 2 1

*Architect Robert A. M. Stern and associates designed their strikingly postmodern
Owligorical House for an exhibit of birdhouses at the Parrish Museum in Southampton,
New York. Fit for upscale birds-of-a-feather, the house is constructed of painted wood,
patinated copper, and gold leaf, over leaf.*

For John, always

ACKNOWLEDGMENTS

In writing this book, I was pleased to have the help of so many people. Special thanks must go to all the artists, craftspeople, and designers who shared their stories and their time. Thanks, too, to Roger Rose, Alice Hoffman, Aarne Anton, Susie Fisk-Stern, Steven Shapiro, Jean Voight, and Judy Heidemann for sharing their knowledge and enthusiasm. As I have before, I thank Mary Forsell for her deft editorial touch, Andrew Baseman for his unerring eye, Keonaona Peterson for her enthusiasm and suggestions, and Marta Hallett and Ellen Milionis for that uncommon business commodity, friendship. Jill Hamilton deserves many thanks for pinch-hitting under pressure, as do Enid Rivera and Linda Greer for their help in many ways, large and small. Finally, thanks to Diane for being a fine researcher and an even finer sister.

CONTENTS

GIVE THEM SHELTER

No object is more emblematic of domesticity on the one hand, or more representative of our interdependence with wild things on the other, than a birdhouse. Physically it symbolizes all the virtues of home—safety, enclosure, stability; functionally, though, it represents a longing to bring untamed nature into our lives. When we put a bird in a cage, we are exercising our dominion over it. But when we set out a birdhouse, we acknowledge that our lawns, gardens, and backyards

The classic aviary, which first became popular in the late sixteenth century, provides charming housing for birds you wish to keep close to home.

can never belong to us alone. The birds, finally, have the right of eminent domain.

Of course, these aren't likely to be among our thoughts when we make the decision to acquire a birdhouse. Indeed, there are probably as many explanations for the appeal of birdhouses as there are birdhouse fanciers. Nevertheless, a few compelling ones stand out.

Since the Renaissance, we have been enamored of miniature houses . . . with the whimsy of barns and cottages and castles no higher than a footstool . . . with tiny chimneys and dormers and cupolas and every imaginable element of human architecture shrunk to sparrow size. Another possible explanation for our love of birdhouses is offered by California folk-art dealer Judy Heidemann: "They make us laugh," she observes.

What could be more charming, after all, than designer Michael Ridel's gray-shingled Cape Cod cottage, with its second-story dormers and hinged front door? What could be wittier than Randy Sewell's all-American diner, complete with red "neon" sign? Or more appealing than a weathered lighthouse that served for decades as a beacon for birds in search of shelter? No wonder that birdhouses, old and new, have emerged as among the most collectible examples of folk art. Many older houses even carry with them mementos of former use—feathers stuck under the eaves, abandoned nests, entry holes pecked smooth by generations of avian inhabitants. Even in an urban living room, a birdhouse reminds us of the freer world *out there*.

While most birdhouses are essentially architectural, many are wild expressions of the quirky personalities who created them. Imagine the now nameless craftsman who fashioned a six-foot birdhouse in the shape of Maine. Or the tinsmith who cut a wren-

Tenements ringing New York City's Clinton Community Garden inspired this very urban birdhouse, designed by conceptual artist Laura Foreman.

A vintage house for gregarious martins, crafted in Maine, features forty-eight separate "apartments" for communal living.

size hole in a larger-than-life metal acorn. For decades, most birdhouses were built by dedicated amateurs who loved birds as much as they did their craft. When we rescue a well-used birdhouse from a vine-covered fencepost, or bid on one at a gallery auction, we acknowledge the spirit and creativity of these anonymous artisans.

The Victorians promoted the notion of the yard and garden as an extension of the house itself, as much a living space as the parlor and the dining room—an idea that, happily, has been revived over the past decade. More and more, we look to decorate our gardens as we do our houses, with perennial beds replacing wallpaper and carpeting, and Lutyens benches and Jekyll urns taking the place of sofas and end tables. As objects of charm and beauty, birdhouses have become the most popular of garden ornaments. Like the designs of the gardens themselves, they can be elegant, taking the form of a whitewashed dovecote rising above a bed of Japanese iris, or informal, such as a rustic barrel-shaped birdhouse on whose carved-wood stand clambers a profusion of white clematis. Birdhouses have a host of personalities. They can make us gasp—imagine a sweeping greensward punctuated by a single towering martin house. Just as readily, they can bring smiles, especially such simply lighthearted designs as a wren house fashioned from an old boot in a children's topiary garden. In addition, they add an invaluable decorative dividend, in the form of bright plumage, not to mention brilliant birdsong.

Even if their man-made abodes weren't so appealing, we would surely welcome birds into our yards and gardens. Throughout human history, birds have delighted and fascinated us. Paleolithic artists painted their images onto cave walls in Europe, Africa, and Australia. In various guises, and in numerous cultures, birds were emblems of ancient fertility goddesses. The ancient Egyptians gave their deities the form of birds, from Thoth, the ibis-headed god of knowledge, to the falcon-headed Horus, lord of the sky. Seagoing petrels are often assumed to owe their name to St. Peter, for their apparent ability to walk on water. And bluebirds have long been a symbol of uncomplicated pleasure. There are few sights so charming as one of these lovely birds gently nudging her nestlings out of the birdhouse for their first shaky attempts at flight.

In our urbanized, technological age, many of us are unaware of the beneficial nature of birds. Agricultural societies through the ages, however, have sought to attract birds as an astonishingly effective means of pest control and a ready source of fertilizer. The graceful bluebird is a voracious consumer of beetles, grasshoppers, and caterpillars; sparrows happily gobble up wasps and other winged pests; and owls and kestrels exhibit an unflagging appetite for rats and mice. Praising the owl's prodigious rodent-catching abilities, the nineteenth-century naturalist Charles Waterton wrote, "I have offered it hospitality and protection on account of its persecutions, and for its many services to me." Perhaps the most dramatic example of birdly beneficence took place in Utah in 1848. That was the year horrified Mormon colonists watched their crops being consumed by hordes of crickets; there seemed no way to stem

An architectural birdhouse adds sculptural interest to a country-style china cabinet. Overleaf, a bevy of martin houses dresses up the front yard of a country cottage in Bee, Nebraska.

the destruction until the fortuitous arrival of thousands of hungry gulls, who saved the crops and rescued the Mormons from potential starvation. A monument to the gulls still stands in Salt Lake City.

Egyptian farmers have kept pigeons for centuries in what may be the world's most spectacular birdhouses. The towering mud-and-straw pigeon cotes, which still rise above the Egyptian landscape like monoliths from another world, provide a nearly limitless supply of nutrient-rich fertilizer—an agricultural requisite in a country where three or more crops are reaped every year from the same acreage. Indeed, there was a time when an Egyptian without a pigeon cote could kiss his chances for matrimony goodbye; prospective fathers-in-law regarded him as a man without a future.

Closer to home, those of us struggling to maintain a chemical-free lawn would do well to attract the sparrow, a bird known to gorge itself on weed seeds.

The American naturalist John Muir called birds the "buoys and lighthouses of nature." In their success (or failure) at surviving assaults to the environment, they represent a highly accurate gauge of nature's state of health, warning us of troubles that may still remain unseen and unheeded. One environmental crisis that can no longer be ignored—and the most compelling reason for setting out a birdhouse—is the dramatic loss of habitat that has threatened dozens of species of birds with extinction. The causes are complex and varied: increased use of pesticides by farmers and homeowners, clearing of forest land in the name of development, forestry practices that result in the cutting of hardwoods in favor of faster-growing pine, the pruning of orchards, and the introduction of foreign species. In 1890 and 1891, for example, the American Acclimatization Society, determined to ensure that every bird mentioned in the works of William Shakespeare should flap its wings over American soil, released one hundred European starlings in New York's Central Park. Though the act was well intentioned, today these prolific and aggressive birds have extended their range throughout virtually all of the contiguous forty-eight states, depriving other, less assertive birds—bluebirds and martins among them—of nesting sites. Over the past century, the eastern bluebird population has quite literally been decimated by loss of habitat.

The erection of birdhouses and nesting boxes can have a dramatic effect. In 1989 Hurricane Hugo ravaged the southeastern coast of the United States, leaving unparalleled destruction in its wake. Among the lesser-known casualties of the storm were 63 percent of the red-cockaded woodpeckers in South Carolina's Francis Marion National Forest. After the deluge, the U.S. Forest Service installed nesting boxes, providing shelter for the birds that had managed to ride out the storm. Two years later the Forest Service counted nearly one thousand woodpeckers in Francis Marion—twice as many, it is believed, as would have survived without the nesting boxes.

Backyard birders, too, can make a difference. Each birdhouse or nesting box erected represents not just the survival of a pair of birds but an opportunity to reproduce and increase the species. It is a simple way of repaying the birds for their countless gifts to us.

So what, ultimately, is a birdhouse? It can be as simple as a recycled detergent bottle, as elaborate as a Bavarian castle in miniature. It might be constructed of bent twigs, old barn wood, or whitewashed cedar. It may look like a Victorian cottage or a railroad car or the Leaning Tower of Pisa. Whatever form it assumes, however, it will always remain a symbol of the beneficence of nature and the extraordinary beauty of birds. With luck, it will also represent the human ability to coexist with and preserve the wild gifts that surround us.

1

BIRDHOUSE BASICS

It's one of those rare days in late winter, when the weather is unseasonably warm and the breeze is full of the smell of spring. Suddenly, it's possible to imagine the world in bloom again and to conjure up the sound of birdsong—just the kind of day that gets people to thinking about putting up a birdhouse or two. Inspired by the balmy weather and the promise of chirping visitors, many of us rush out to satisfy that end-of-winter urge without the least understanding of what

A red, white, and blue "lighthouse" does double duty, providing housing for the birds and gentle entertainment for their human neighbors.

we're buying. No matter how much it pleases us aesthetically, a birdhouse is first and foremost a home for birds. If the house is to be used outdoors, it needs to meet certain standards to be safe for its occupants. And as pretty as your yard may look to *you*, it may not be hospitable to the avian tenants you hope to attract.

To Each Bird a House

The most important thing to know about birdhouses is that different models attract different species of birds, depending on such structural factors as the size of the entrance hole, the depth of the interior, and the height at which the house is mounted or hung. (See the table on page 73 for dimensions and other specifics.)

Don't expect to find a house to suit literally every bird: the only birds that will inhabit man-made houses are cavity nesters—such species as wrens, nuthatches, and starlings, whose natural nesting places are hollow logs or tree limbs. (This still leaves you with upwards of fifty potential species, depending on where you live, as well as the beam nesters.)

The most common commercially produced birdhouses are designed for small birds such as wrens, chickadees, and titmice. Indeed, wrens—the squatters of the bird world—will nest virtually anywhere: old boots and shoes, junked automobile radiators, empty flowerpots, mailboxes, or fishing creels. Wrens have even made their home in a pair of blue jeans left out too long on a laundry line. And wrens are prodigious—some might even say *compulsive*—nest-builders. A male wren may build a half-dozen nests, most of them dummies to dupe or warn off other birds in the area. When the female wren deigns to move in, she often destroys her mate's earnest work, rebuilding the nest to suit her personal fancy.

A tufted titmouse makes its home in this simple but well-constructed house.

Martins in the eastern United States nest mainly in groups. The special features of this vintage two-story martin house—maroon trim and irregularly placed entrance holes—raise it above the ordinary.

Though bluebirds will sometimes nest in houses designed for wrens, it's best to buy a house built to suit their particular needs. (For dimensions of a typical bluebird house, see page 73.) If you're serious about attracting bluebirds—and with the drastic decline in bluebird habitat, everyone who *can* be *should* be—mount the houses four to seven feet off the ground in an open area, preferably at the edge of woodlands (a long fence row is ideal). For each acre or so of land, expect to attract one nesting pair.

Doves, pigeons, and martins generally prefer to nest in colonies. Dovecotes, which attract both doves and pigeons, are traditionally cylindrical, and can range in height from one foot to twelve feet and up. Martin houses usually feature four to twenty-four separate "apartments," though martins will also happily nest in hollowed gourds, massed together and strung from high tree limbs or posts. The gourds should be far enough apart so that a strong gust won't knock them together.

You can also buy houses built specifically for larger birds such as screech, barn, and saw-whet owls, as well as kestrels, flickers, and red-bellied woodpeckers. Wood ducks, too, will nest in man-made houses, especially if you place them near a shallow body of water incorporating islands, snags, and some form of natural cover. To make the duck houses hospitable to their prospective tenants, line the bottom of each cavity with soft debris—wood shavings, soft pine bark, and the like.

A red-shingled wren house at left is suspended from the sturdy branches of a white pine. At right, clay bottles like these have been housing small birds since American Colonial days.

The "porches" ringing this purple martin house, left, keep baby birds from tumbling to the ground. Though it won't attract partridges to the Bradford pear tree at right, a cheerfully painted wren house offers shelter to a variety of small species.

Beam nesters—birds such as phoebes, robins, and barn swallows that typically nest in tree crotches—can be enticed to nest on man-made "shelves." These are generally simple structures, open on two sides, with a shelflike floor and a slanting roof. The particular pleasure of shelf houses derives from their very simplicity and openness: they make it easy to observe the birds' ingenious handi-work—cupped nests plastered together with a mixture of mud and straw—as well as their eventual progeny.

Materials

The best birdhouses are made of wood (cedar, pine, and fir are all good choices), which serves as an excellent insulator and stands up well to the elements. Avoid wood treated with preservatives or insecticides, however. Houses of cement and terra cotta are also generally hospitable to birds, but *never* buy a metal house: it will be

stiflingly hot in summer, and fledglings cannot climb its smooth surface to leave the nest.

Paint is another matter. While birdhouse interiors should always be left unpainted, stained or painted exteriors are fine, as long as the paint is water-based. Common bird lore warns against the use of brightly colored paint, since birds are said to be frightened by vivid colors (the sole exception being martins, who seem to prefer the heat-deflecting quality of white houses). The observations of many backyard birders may refute this claim, however: Georgia artist Randy Sewell, for example, whose colorful birdhouses are fashioned after vernacular roadside architecture, says that local birds flock to his neon-blue diners and crimson fireworks stands. Talk to birders in your area and learn of their observations.

Essentials of Good Construction

No one disputes certain birdhouse basics: specifically, the need for ventilation and drainage. Without proper ventilation, fledglings can suffocate; without drainage, they can drown. Every birdhouse should have at least two holes or slats on either side to allow air to circulate. To keep houses rainproof, the roof should overhang the body of the house by at least one-eighth inch (houses with flat roofs should have shallow rain troughs on two sides). Some kind of overhang to protect birds from sun and rain is also recommended. Another important feature is an interior foothold for babies en route to the great outdoors. A series of cleats or horizontal grooves provides excellent purchase for fledgling feet.

Architect Joseph G. Costa designed his "Subirdian" row houses, left, specifically for downy woodpeckers, whose soft plumage and sweet song still recall for him childhood walks through the woods. The Carpenter Gothic birdhouse at right was designed for wrens and chickadees with a taste for Victoriana.

Scouting a Location

Location is as important as size, shape, height, and construction in the overall birdhouse picture—a truism for birders as well as realtors. In general, a birdhouse should be set away from dense foliage but close enough to such natural perches as trees and shrubs. If you've recently landscaped your property, you may have to change the location of the birdhouse as plantings mature. Orientation is less important, as long as the house is properly designed to deflect rain and sun.

Not all birds prefer to nest in the open, however, and some are extremely picky about their neighborhood. Chickadees and titmice, for example, nest in wooded areas, so their houses should be placed within ten to fifteen feet of dense shrubbery. Purple martins prefer a combination of open fields and water; if you don't have both nearby, the best martin house in the world won't meet this species' standards. Tree swallows, too, nest near bodies of water, such as lakes, ponds, and even swimming pools.

Though houses for smaller birds can be suspended from a branch or beam (or, in the case of gregarious wrens, right from the eaves of your house), larger birdhouses should be mounted on metal or wooden posts set in concrete or a rock-lined hole. Most manufacturers supply information on how to mount their houses, but whatever you do, make sure the mounting is secure; if the house topples, eggs can be smashed and fledglings injured. Some smaller birdhouses are designed to be mounted against a tree. To protect the bark, place a layer of rubber between tree and house.

SAFETY FIRST

In your backyard, as in the wild, predators present a constant danger to baby birds, so houses should be mounted at least five feet from the ground. If cats and squirrels are a problem, try attaching an inverted funnel-shaped piece of metal to the pole, eighteen inches from the ground (the funnel should extend ten inches from the pole on all sides). To hungry raccoons, eggs and baby birds represent a springtime delicacy. Attaching a three-quarter-inch block of wood over the hole—with a hole drilled in the wood to match that of the entryway—will keep nestlings safely away from the reach of even the most rapacious raccoon.

The greatest threat to nesting birds, however, comes not from backyard predators but from other birds. Starlings and many sparrows commonly move in on established birds, sometimes even building their nests on top of the eggs of former inhabitants. If the house you buy comes with an exterior perch, remove it—perches are unnecessary and serve only as an invitation to nest competitors.

TIMING

Flush with enthusiasm, many novice backyard birders eagerly put out their first house, only to find no takers. This doesn't necessarily mean they've done something wrong. It can take several years to attract birds to your birdhouse—many birds, in fact, seem to prefer slightly weathered houses. On the other hand, there may be something amiss. Timing, for example, is extremely important. Though houses can be set out as late as early July in northern climates, the optimum time is early spring, when most migratory birds begin to return to their summer habitats. In North America this means January for the deep South, February for the Middle Atlantic states, and March for the northern United States and Canada. In the British Isles and Europe, February is also the optimal time.

BACKYARD HABITATS

The general habitat your backyard provides is crucial to attracting and maintaining a varied selection of birds. In addition to shelter, all birds require food, water, and cover. If even one of these is absent, you may find yourself the owner of an unoccupied birdhouse. Fortunately, all three are easy to provide.

A bird feeder is the simplest means of providing food, and has the added advantage of showing you exactly which birds will nest in your area. Like houses, feeders don't always attract birds the instant they're set out, but patience will be well rewarded. Placed near a window, a bird feeder provides countless hours of pleasure (around our house, we refer to it as "cat TV"). In late summer, some birds will even bring their young to the feeder with them.

Nuthatches, chickadees, finches, and titmice prefer hanging feeders, while sparrows, towhees, doves, and cardinals like to feed on the ground. Since birds aren't the neatest of diners, normal spillage will usually satisfy ground feeders. You might also set out a basket or a shallow dish with drainage holes. By far the most popular food for the widest variety of birds is sunflower seeds, but cracked corn and mixed seed are favorites as well. Insect-eaters such as woodpeckers are attracted to suet, peanut butter, and bird cakes; there are many fine suet feeders on the market, but a mesh bag, such as the kind used for onions, mounted to a tree trunk will work just as well. It's best to avoid bread as a staple, since it's low in essential nutrients and is metabolized too quickly to provide energy to fight the cold. It's also been known to attract unwanted rodents.

Before feeders, of course, birds depended on nature to provide them with sustenance, often in the form of fruit-, seed-, and nut-bearing trees, shrubs, vines, and flowers. Some of the best natural sources of bird food are dogwoods, for their autumn fruit; berry bushes of all kinds, including sumacs; flowering crab apple; sunflowers and burning bush, for their seeds; and, especially, Virginia creeper, a prolific vine whose fruit attracts dozens of species of birds.

Trees and shrubs also provide perches and natural cover. For additional cover, set out your Christmas trees rather than consigning them to landfill. And consider keeping a corner of your yard "wild"—far from meticulous, birds prefer a little mess, in the form of brush piles, dead tree limbs, and tangled weed patches.

If your yard lacks a natural source of water, a birdbath is inexpensive, attractive, and eminently practical. Set it up in an open area, but make sure that a perch of some kind is no more than ten feet away. In warmer weather, birds are especially fond of drip-baths, which can be as simple as a water-filled pail with a small hole in the bottom, hung above the birdbath.

Don't forget, too, that birds need an abundance of nest materials. Each spring, provide them with nesting materials—yarn, cotton, pet and human hair, straw, grass, twigs, strips of paper or cloth, feathers, down, bark, moss, even cellophane. Make sure, however, that no strand is longer than about four inches; birds can entangle themselves in longer strands. You can simply leave these raw materials out in the open, or buy or improvise a box for them. Mount it near a window and you guarantee yourself the fun of watching an avian architect at work.

WINTER CLEANUP

Having enjoyed your birdhouse all spring and summer, you'll wake one day to an autumnal chill and the sight of turning leaves. The nesting season ends by late fall, even for nonmigratory birds, and this is the time for birdhouse maintenance. An essential feature of any birdhouse is a removable wall, floor, or roof for easy cleaning. (If you're lucky enough to have martins, make sure the houses are mounted on poles that can be lowered.) Take out old nests and debris, and scrub the interior with a stiff brush. If parasites are present, use strong soap and water and rinse well. Avoid insect spray unless absolutely necessary.

To keep nature's ravages to a minimum, bring the house indoors if you can. This is a good time to make repairs and to repaint, if

The quintessential martin house, painted a traditional white, rises like a beacon above a rural farmhouse.

either is called for. If the house will be wintering outside, cover the hole to discourage mice from taking up residence.

Don't forget to keep the feeder well stocked. Overwintering birds such as chickadees and titmice need the extra food now more than they did when the days were long and balmy, and they'll be more likely to inhabit your birdhouses come spring if you provide them with winter sustenance. Another way to encourage birds to stick around is to provide them with a roosting box, a large houselike structure with interior roosts for a number of birds.

Well cared for, a birdhouse can be a perennial source of pleasure and discovery. Like many backyard birders, however, you may find that one isn't enough. If you have room for more, by all means indulge your enthusiasm: your family and neighbors won't complain, and the birds will sing your praises.

A rustic feeder not only adds beauty to the winter garden, but helps support dozens of species of overwintering birds.

2

....

RUSTIC ABODES

Every birdhouse, no matter what its design, possesses an element of rusticity. Strip it of its architectural finery and you have a structure that was designed to live—and support life—in nature. Given a few years' use and exposure to the elements, even the most elegant architectonic birdhouse begins to take on the patina of the out-of-doors. Sun and rain blister its paint, revealing the natural wood beneath. Birds smooth the contours of its entrance hole as they come and go. Bits of

The charm of a simple wooden birdhouse, mounted against an old tree, is enhanced by the twinings of wisteria.

The creative sleight-of-hand of Alabama's Reverend Benjamin Franklin Perkins turns a simple gourd house, left, into a small work of art. Center, an ethereal bent-twig birdhouse, crafted by furniture designer Clifton Monteith, seems ready to take wing. The basic vintage house at right has a slightly dilapidated but comfortable quality.

nesting material find their way into cracks and crevices. What was once the perfect replica of an eighteenth-century mansion now looks like the home for wild things that it was intended to be.

Given their predilection for the natural look, the birds undoubtedly prefer it that way. Perhaps that's why some of the most successful birdhouses are rustic by design. Incorporating natural, often weathered, materials, rustic birdhouses most closely resemble the wild homes of cavity-nesting birds, such as tree trunks and hollow logs.

Basic Boxes

The most basic rustic houses are simple stand-ins for what nature no longer provides in sufficient abundance. Thanks largely to the efforts of such wildlife advocates as the National Audubon Society and local natural history societies, plain boxes of cedar and pine now dot the landscape from southern Florida to the Pacific Northwest, housing birds whose habitats have been severely reduced by development and deforestation. The North American Bluebird Society, for example, has done enormous work in spreading their message: without human intervention, the beautiful Eastern bluebird will most likely vanish from fields and backyards forever. Delaware's celebrated Winterthur Museum maintains twenty-five cedar-shingled bluebird houses in their sprawling gardens, with spectacular results—now the lilting call of bluebirds wafts above the copses of azalea and rhododendron all spring and summer long.

Other successful rustic "housing projects" include boxes for owls, kestrels, and wood ducks. Because they feed on rodents and large insects, both owls and kestrels are important allies in the pest-control war, and are a good deal safer than chemical pesticides. Communities across North America have set out hundreds of the spacious boxes to help fight rodent infestations. (One of the most publicized uses of owl boxes was in New York's Central Park, where the rat population was booming in spite of repeated applications of poison; unfortunately, the attractive owl boxes proved too strong a temptation to human city dwellers, and most of them were stolen before the owls could get a foothold.)

Though vegetarian wood ducks won't do much in the area of vermin control, the presence of these elegant birds—the most colorful ducks in North America—is sufficient justification for setting out a duck house or two, if the environment is hospitable (see page 73). They may be migratory, but wood ducks are homebodies at heart: a female wood duck will return to the same area—and very likely the same house—year after year.

Handcrafted in England, the charming thatched-roof birdhouse at top evokes classic Celtic wattle-and-daub architecture. Bottom, a rough-hewn bluebird house from the American Primitive collection takes its name literally.

Organic Architecture

No one knows for sure what the earliest birdhouses looked like, but they were probably functional affairs, built of natural, unfinished materials. Their builders' intent was certainly less aesthetic than practical; people living in close harmony with nature know that there exists no better means of insect control than a clutch of songbirds. On the North American continent, the first birdhouses were probably hollowed-out gourds, strung from trees and poles by Native Americans of the Southeast to attract purple martins. When the European settlers arrived, they took up the practice, and it continues to this day, especially in the rural South. Hung together by the dozens, these gourd houses are still intended to house

The basic bluebird house at left is equipped with a baffle to foil potential predators. Center and right, a thatched-roof coconut and a hollowed log provide organic shelter for small birds. At far right, gourds grouped to attract martins take on a pleasing, sculptural aspect.

Michael Ridel's "Wood Shed" has the appeal of a hand-hewn country homestead.

nesting martins, but they also attract other small birds, including titmice, bluebirds, nuthatches, swallows, house sparrows, fly-catchers, and wrens.

The tradition of gourd houses has weathered the centuries be-cause the gourds suit their purpose perfectly. But the houses also possess natural charm: a single gourd, strung from an overhead branch, has an almost whimsical quality; strung in groups, they take on the look of modern sculpture. Indeed, in the hands of artists like Alabama's Reverend Benjamin Franklin Perkins, they *are* works of art. A self-taught painter and preacher, Reverend Perkins decorates his "churches for the birds" with patriotic and religious motifs, including flags, the Statue of Liberty, and bits of writing, all in a striking palette of red, white, and blue. Though highly embellished, the gourds reflect a reverence for nature that keeps them well in the realm of the rustic.

Traditional Rustics

While some European immigrants to North America were setting out hollow gourds like their tribal neighbors, others fashioned bird bottles of glazed clay. The small bottles were fixed to the clapboards of colonial houses and provided hospitable shelter to wrens and other gregarious birds. (They continue to attract feathered tenants even today in Virginia's Colonial Williamsburg.) Other basic houses were fashioned from weathered barrels and buckets. Aarne Anton, a New York dealer in American folk art, found a particularly compelling barrel-house in Elmira, New York. Built in the state penitentiary in the early part of this century, the house is purely functional save for a painted finial of turned wood on the top. Even thus unadorned, it undoubtedly brought a small element of freedom to the dark confines of the prison.

The Nesting Instinct

Some rustic houses are modeled not after logs or tree trunks but the nests woven inside of them. Basket birdhouses have been an important part of the southern handicraft tradition for generations, and they can still be found nailed to fenceposts and barn sidings throughout the South. Woven skeps—traditionally used to house colonies of bees—were also modified to make charming birdhouses, a trend being revived by the firm Country Originals.

Malcolm Wells, a Cape Cod architect with a special interest in birdhouses, has designed a "living" birdhouse—a wooden nesting shelf covered with a mound of topsoil, compost, and mulch, and surrounded by twigs, grasses, and blooming wildflowers. The most "natural" of rustic birdhouses, it derives its inspiration from the birds' own unique architecture.

Taking their cue from the "plaster" houses built by robins and swallows, German "wood-crete" birdhouses are made, as their name suggests, from a combination of wood and concrete. Hung from a branch or fixed to the trunk of a tree, they have a rough "make-do" charm that belies the efficiency (and bird-friendliness) of their construction.

Rustic by Design

In the realm of birdhouse architecture, as in contemporary design in general, rustic doesn't necessarily connote simple or unadorned. A whole generation of designers are creating rustic birdhouses that deftly blend utility and beauty. Reflecting a growing environmental awareness, these designers not only use natural materials, they often put cast-off materials to new use. Recycling, in fact, has long been a traditional element of birdhouse construction; for years, local folk artists have used old barn wood, discarded license plates, and other found objects to create unique pieces of avian architecture. (More examples of this type of design can be found in Chapter Four, "Fanciful and Fantastic.")

Randy Ouzts, who once designed windows for Gucci and Bergdorf Goodman in New York, now turns out extraordinary rustic birdhouses in his North Carolina studio. While his basic raw material isn't recycled per se, it was, until recently, considered worse than trash by most of his southern neighbors: Ouzts's elegant birdhouses and feeders are fashioned of kudzu, the prodigious vine that is literally engulfing the southern United States in its twisted

Whimsical details of rural architecture inspired these birdhouses from the design firm Garden Source. On each model roofs, windows, portals, and chimneys are harmonized to create a miniature replica of the real thing.

tendrils. Woven into a birdhouse, kudzu is transformed from a vegetable pest into something ethereal and surprisingly nestlike, and birds find it uniquely hospitable.

Sam and Pat Grove, husband-and-wife designers in Spicewood, Texas, construct whimsical and architectural rustic birdhouses from cedar trees felled by local developers. Everything on the houses, including architectural flourishes, was at one time destined for the landfill—driftwood, bits of fencing wire removed from neighboring ranches, cans scavenged from the trash of a local school cafeteria. Birds' nests being the apotheosis of found art, the Groves' designs seem particularly appropriate to their function.

The wild and whimsical birdhouses sold at Growingthings, in Brooklyn, New York, might have been decorated by delirious robins: their fanciful ornamentation includes acorns, balls from the sweet-gum tree, and pine cones. Larry Kenosha's graceful birdhouse is woven of native Minnesota basswood and trimmed with local red willow; bits of sawn popple stick give it the look of an otherworldly log cabin. A Native American, Kenosha learned from a tribal elder to gather materials with respect; one night in a dream he saw his birdhouse, and after two years of architectural refinements, it found its way to such citadels of retail design as New York's Whitney Museum Shop.

In southern England, the artisans of English Thatch turn out some of the most enchanting rustic birdhouses ever to grace a country garden or suburban backyard. Made with authentic Devon thatch, the houses have a rough-hewn architectural charm, incorporating such features as the traditional "English eyebrow" arch.

Perhaps the most extraordinary rustic birdhouses come from the hand of Michigan furniture designer Clifton Monteith. Crafted mostly of bent willow and cedar, the birdhouses are highly sculptural, each incorporating a complex series of planes and curves. A Monteith birdhouse readily brings to mind the grace of birds in flight—though in fact, most of his houses go to collectors who keep them safely away from real birds and the out-of-doors.

Nevertheless, rustic birdhouses have a special affinity for wooded landscapes and countrified backyards. The same birch-log house that adds charm to the shaded porch of a lakeside cabin seems right at home hanging from the eaves of a suburban toolshed. And because they blend naturally with the landscape, rustic birdhouses don't need to stand alone. If a yard is large enough, dozens of them can decorate tree trunks, fence posts, even the sides of outbuildings.

Not every environment can support a towering cluster of martin-house gourds on twenty-foot poles, but a half-dozen gourds, suspended from the spokes of a recycled wagon wheel, make for instant sculpture even in a garden of modest proportion. And wooded or not, there is no yard so small that it couldn't accommodate the charm of a single diminutive woven wren house. The wrens, if they could, would certainly agree.

3

ARCHITECTURAL OPTIONS

Over the years, birdhouses have assumed every conceivable form, from simple wooden boxes bereft of decoration to human figures whose open mouths served as entrance holes, to futuristic plastic "yo-yos," designed in the early 1960s to complement modern architecture. But one trend has remained constant: when we build for the birds, more often than not, *house* is where the heart is. Attribute it to anthropomorphism, or the gentle sense of whimsy that birds

But for its scale, this shuttered mansion, complete with cupola and widow's walk, might have been built for the family of a Nantucket sea captain.

Dating from 1866, this architectural birdhouse wonder, above, was forged by the Miller Iron Works of Providence, Rhode Island. The cast-iron form ensured its survival well beyond the nineteenth century. Also built to endure, a stalwart dovecote—once the ultimate status symbol—lends distinction to an English garden, right.

seem to inspire, but the vast majority of birdhouses have always taken their architectural cue from human habitations.

Dovecotes and Martin Houses

As early as the thirteenth century, Europeans were building architectural birdhouses on a grand scale. From the late Middle Ages through the early Victorian era, the predominant European birdhouse was the dovecote, a cottage-size structure, usually of stone, built to house the pigeons that were a staple of the European diet. (Some surviving cotes are so large that they have been comfortably converted to house people.) Like the ancient dovecote at Athelhampton, England, and the two eighteenth-century pigeon houses built for the Parlange plantation in southern Louisiana, many were simple rounded stone structures with conical roofs—the traditional "pepper-pot" shape.

In the nineteenth and early twentieth centuries, dovecotes were generally downsized to suit smaller, middle-class gardens, but they still retained some distinctive architectural features. The British garden designer Gertrude Jekyll, a former painter, did much to

promote the dovecote as garden ornament not just for the wealthy, but for the average citizen. J. P. White's Pyghtle Works of Bedford, England, supplied decorative dovecotes to bird fanciers around the world, and the company's charming catalogue illustrations are emblematic of the prevailing styles in dovecote and garden design: an oak barrel with a conical shingled roof marks the pathway in a country garden; a stately rectangular pigeon cote with its lead-covered mansard-style roof stands sentry over the manicured hedges of a formal landscape in the French style.

Just as dovecotes had their beginnings in rural, agricultural settings, so did martin houses. Unlike the pigeons who resided in traditional dovecotes, however, martins weren't valued as food or fertilizer producers, but as highly efficient insectivores; one purple martin may consume as many as 250,000 mosquitoes and other insects in a single season, reason enough for any farmer to put up a martin house or two. The basic martin house looks a bit like a typical midwestern farmhouse: a multistoried white building with a pitched roof and numerous "windows" opening onto individual nesting compartments. (In the eastern United States, martins prefer to nest en masse, but their cousins in the deserts of the Southwest remain solitary nesters. In the Pacific Northwest the martins eschew birdhouses to nest in large colonies on cliffs.) Perhaps the most extraordinary example of martin housing can be found in Griggsville, Illinois, the self-proclaimed martin capital of the world. In the center of town rises a martin skyscraper with room for six hundred or so of the well-loved migrants.

Architect George F. Henschel found the model for his painted-wood birdhouse in the Bedford, New York, Free Library building, built in 1807—whose renovation, not coincidentally, he shepherded.

Elements of Style

Birdhouses have been in vogue since the sixteenth century, but they reached their height of expression during the Victorian era—an age marked by its celebration of the domestic virtues and an unprecedented enthusiasm for the idea of *home*. From the nineteenth century on, birdhouse architects turned out thousands of miniature residences, some primitive, others nearly palatial.

Typical of folk art, architectural birdhouses were constructed of whatever materials could be scrounged or put to reuse, such as old crates and barrels, toothpicks, Popsicle sticks, and wood pulled from abandoned barns or tumbledown fences. Architectural and other details might be provided by chunks of broken glass, soda-pop caps, wooden guitar picks, balls of tinfoil, glitter or sand (for rooftop snow), or paint. In the collection of New York's American Primitive Gallery is a red-and-white cabin birdhouse whose "logs" were fashioned entirely from wooden fishing lures.

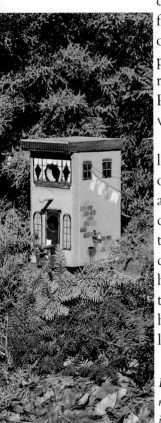

Even the most basic architectural houses featured some kind of loving detail, whether it was a row of scalloped shingles on an otherwise plain wood roof, a small whittled chimney, or windows and doors painted in a rainbow palette. Many birdhouses, of course, were as elaborate as the full-scale architecture that inspired them. Victorian domiciles, loaded with gingerbread, were especially popular and continue to be; an ornate Victorian-style birdhouse in the American Primitive collection was made in this century by Chippewa Indians, whose models may have been the houses of Scandinavians who settled near the reservation in the late 1800s. Other Victorian-style birdhouses found their inspiration

Despite its metropolitan roots, Joyce Olsen's "Brooklyn Brownstone," left, seems very much at home in a lush garden setting. At right, a shady verandah and gingerbread trim invite birds and their admirers to this charming avian summerhouse.

Birdhouses have been fashioned after every conceivable human edifice, from Victorian Gothic cottages to quaint country churches to pillared municipal buildings—all of which make an appearance in the not-so-urban sprawl exhibited in this roadside display.

in patterns printed in popular magazines and newspapers from the 1920s on; though surviving examples share nearly identical architecture, most have been distinctively personalized with paint, trim, and appliqués.

Regional Designs

More modest houses, too, served as the creative spark for birdhouse builders. Many birdhouses were small-scale recreations of local architecture or specific buildings. A white "saltbox" birdhouse built in Maine in the 1940s boasts a painted-brick foundation and chimneys, a shingled roof, red-painted trim, and a matching red-and-white fence; it is the very model of a New England house of the period. A permanent fixture in Jean Voight's shop, Dovetails, is a large birdhouse bearing the distinctive architectural details of Virginia's Eastern Shore. Indeed, birdhouses come in as many architectural styles as the human habitations that inspired them—Adirondack split-log lodges, squat southwestern-style "adobe" houses, San Francisco Victorians as lacy and lush as wedding cakes.

In my own New Jersey neighborhood stands a wonderful, slightly ramshackle Victorian house with a gabled roof and a spacious wraparound porch; before you reach the front steps, you find yourself seeing double, in the form of a miniature version of the same house. The most distinctive difference, aside from scale, arises from the tufts of straw protruding from the tiny "doorway." Such architectural replicas were common among the house-proud Victorians as well as their twentieth-century descendants. But other birdhouse builders chose grander, more public homes for their models: replicas of the White House and Thomas Jefferson's Mon-

Drawing on the English tradition of agricultural architecture, John P. Meyer designed his "Wrenpost" to be in harmony with its environment.

ticello have provided shelter to generations of birds regardless of political persuasion. One artisan—perhaps a recent immigrant still harboring poignant memories of his homeland—modeled a martin house after the Leaning Tower of Pisa.

The architectural urge didn't end with houses, of course. Bird-houses more often than not were built by country dwellers, and they reflected the full gamut of rural architecture—barns, silos, country churches, lighthouses. Judy Heidemann, whose California shop, Wild Goose Chase, specializes in folk-art houses of all kinds, remembers with great fondness a farm-birdhouse consisting of barn, silo, and a farmhouse modeled after the farmer's own.

Their country pedigree notwithstanding, architectural bird-houses were by no means limited to the rural. Folk art has always been distinguished by the fertile imaginations of its practitioners, and birdhouse art is no exception. One New England martin house was modeled after an elaborate Bavarian castle, with Gothic tracery, carved-wood turrets, and a bell tower with a tiny working bell.

Contemporary Trends

Today, as in the nineteenth century, birdhouse designers continue to find inspiration in domestic architecture. Sam Scovil, Jr., of Maine's Backshore Woodworks, builds elegantly streamlined bird-houses that are, first and foremost, for the birds; like many a contemporary architect, his priorities are safety, comfort, and beauty, in that order. Though his birdhouses don't try to mimic human architecture, they take their lacy, gingerbread look from the scrolled porches of New England Victorians. Similarly, the Streck family of New Mexico look to the Tex-Mex architecture of towns like Taos and Chimayo for the painted tin and copper details that ornament their wooden birdhouses.

Combining a lifelong fascination with architecture and antiques, artist Michael Ridel creates architectural birdhouses distinguished by the elegance and intricacy of their detailing. He built his first birdhouse after a friend tore down a fifty-year-old fence and offered it to him as firewood. Ridel was entranced by the beautiful, weathered look of the wood, and decided then and there that it would *not* be used for burning. He continues to use recycled materials for his birdhouses—old wood, rusted hinges, glue rather than nails. Turning strictly to American architecture for inspiration, he is especially fond of his Shaker-style birdhouses; the Shakers' extraordinary sense of proportion imbues even these breadbox-size miniatures with a characteristic grace and beauty.

A different kind of grace infuses the unique birdhouses of Lady Slipper Designs. For nearly two decades, the not-for-profit Minnesota co-op has created striking birdhouses from native kiln-dried pine. The houses, painted a reflecting white, resemble architectural prototypes, ranging in style from Victorian and Greek Revival to Georgian and Beaux Arts.

From Bauhaus to Birdhouse

Architectural birdhouses are by no means mired in the previous century. Atlanta, Georgia, artist Randy Sewell finds his inspiration in the quirky roadside buildings that were a part of his peripatetic childhood. Family auto trips took him to places like Dogland and the Reptile Farm; as tourist attractions they were inevitably less exciting than their exotic names, but as architectural inspiration they had staying power. Today Sewell-housed birds nest in, among other places, Crazy Eddie's Fireworks Stand, the Checkerboard Diner, a wood-and-wire Muffler House, and the Reptile Farm of

Laura Foreman's New York City tenement-inspired birdhouse offers multistory habitation for city and country birds alike.

earlier days. Sewell has a special touch for the details that give these buildings their tacky charm. His Foot-Long Hot Dog House, for instance, is topped by a painted-wood wiener and accompanying ruler, with the Os in Hot Dog serving as twin entrance holes.

Frank Lloyd Wright, who had a lifelong interest in garden orna- ment, may or may not have designed a birdhouse or two during his career. If he did, he would be part of a time-honored tradition; Stanford White and Charles Platt, among other architects, found the design of dovecotes and birdhouses a pleasant diversion from the rigors of traditional architecture. Contemporary architects, too, have tried their hand at birdhouse design. In a 1987 show at the Parrish Museum in Southampton, New York, architectural lumi- naries such as Michael Graves and Robert A. M. Stern offered up a striking variety of modern and postmodern avian abodes. Graves's coyly titled Christopher's Wren House is the essence of Post- modernism, with its updated tip of the hat to Greek and Roman- esque architecture. William B. White's Total Aviary Environment is the Guggenheim Museum shrunk to sparrow proportions.

The best architectural birdhouses combine a love of design with a reverence for nature, leavened with a good dose of wit. Certainly, Robert A. M. Stern drew on that wit when he designed his post- modern Owl-i-gorical House, as did the anonymous New England artisan who constructed a wildly swaybacked storybook house during the depths of the Great Depression. By reducing architec- tural design to an avian scale, birdhouse designers create structures that add a whimsical note to the outdoor landscape—and remind us that we humans are not alone in our search for comfortable shelter.

The whitewashed birdhouses from Lady Slipper Designs emphasize purity of architectural form. Here, a Greek revival–style church offers avian sanctuary.

4

FANCIFUL AND FANTASTIC

In Moscow's State Historical Museum stands a peasant couple, their outstretched arms frozen in time, their mouths agape and their eyes wide with what strikes the observer as amused pleasure. Perhaps that amusement derives from the couple's secret identity—they are, in reality, a pair of folk-art birdhouses in disguise, whose hollow heads once sheltered nesting starlings and their hungry broods. Carved a century ago by peasant craftsmen, the wooden figures

Whitey's Fish Campstore, set among the bushes, was obviously designed by an enthusiastic fisherman for his avian tenants.

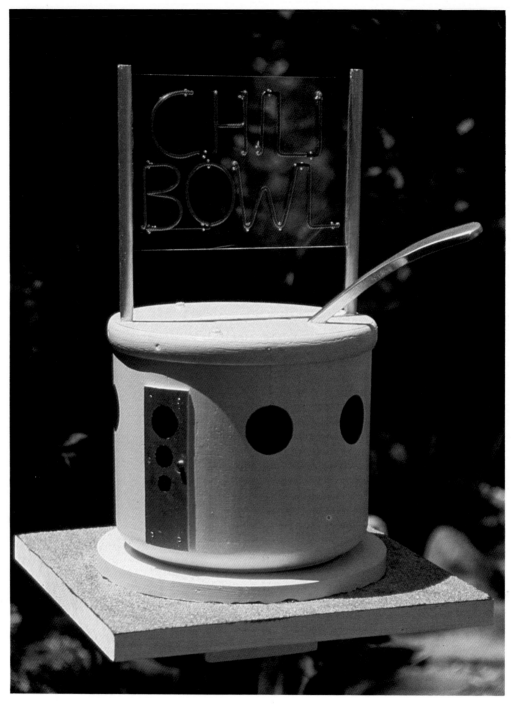

Randy Sewell's eye-catching birdhouses pay homage to the quirky roadside architecture of bygone and fast-disappearing American highways.

represent a long tradition of amateur woodworking in Russia, where forest land was—and continues to be—abundant, and where wood has always been a natural medium for artistic expression.

Birdhouses to Go

Unlike serious architects, the builders of birdhouses have never been hemmed in by zoning regulations, architectural traditions, or considerations of taste and community standards—much to the joy of the builders and their admirers. Though birdhouses are by nature functional, their forms have more often than not been fanciful, reflecting the hobbies, philosophies, and preoccupations of their creators. From the nineteenth century on, one popular theme has been transportation: birdhouses have taken the form of boats, trains, and, beginning in the twentieth century, automobiles and airplanes. The American Primitive collection boasts a trolley and a Chesapeake & Ohio caboose, the latter with such authentic details as movable wheels. Also in the collection are two planes: one is a small-scale but accurate replica of the real thing; the other—typical of folk art—is a wild embellishment on the *idea* of airplane: a towering split-level flying machine with propeller, portholes, and a large running-horse weathervane. Such whimsies were designed not just as shelter for the birds but as decorative, one-of-a-kind lawn ornaments. In the realm of the birdhouse, boats, too, can be true to form or fabulous—from a classic 1930s ocean liner to a fanciful Noah's ark, complete with animals. For bellicose birds, contemporary artist Randy Sewell has even fashioned an ironclad Monitor.

Witty and Whimsical

A common theme, among artists in general and birdhouse builders in particular, is the human or animal form. But while many, perhaps most, artists have approached these forms with reverence, birdhouse architects are clearly drawn to them for the inevitable humor arising from the oddball juxtaposition of form and function. Lee Steen, a Montana craftsman, created dozens of carved-wood birdhouses in the shape of human heads before his death in the 1970s; the birds happily came and went through eye sockets and open mouths.

Contemporary wood-carver Barry Leader carries on the tradition in his Pennsylvania studio. Leader's wooden birdhouses, painted in shockingly vibrant colors, are pure whimsy: a black-and-white cow with flared nostrils, three-dimensional eyelashes, and horns rising atop a peaked roof; a bewhiskered cat with protruding snout; and a "bird house" that is quite literally that—complete with outstretched wings and cartoon-variety legs. In a similar mode, architects James Righter and Kimo Griggs designed a painted-wood bluebird house for the 1987 Parrish Museum show that took off on the idea of "bird"; it featured a highly stylized beak-perch atop a pair of spindly six-foot legs.

Pure Fantasy

Many birdhouses simply defy classification, reflecting the unique imaginative gifts of their creators; long before "serious" art embraced the abstract and the free-form, folk artists were un-selfconsciously turning out wildly abstract objects, birdhouses among them. A rectangular red, white, and blue birdhouse, found in Iowa and probably dating from the 1930s, features a trio of entrance holes that can be closed with movable slats; on each slat is painted a weird, unblinking eye. Another vintage house, dating from around the same period, looks like a wild interpretation of

Vivid colors and flamboyant forms distinguish a fanciful wren house from Arts for the Birds.

L. Frank Baum's Emerald City, a crazy turreted admixture of futurism and Aztec architecture.

Some of the most strikingly original birdhouses have been wrought by self-taught "outsider" artists of the American South, men and women with no formal schooling in the artistic traditions who have nevertheless created works as inspired and exciting as anything that ever hung on museum walls. Willie Massey, for example, was a Kentucky folk artist—in his own words a "trickster"—known for his boldly painted and wildly ornamented avian sculptures and birdhouses. He was a master of the found object: his birdhouses are adorned with birds, snakes, and satellites wrought from fruit crates, twigs, aluminum foil, scrap metal, and whatever else was at hand.

Alabama artist Mose Tolliver, on the other hand, embellishes his birdhouses with paint alone. Indeed, Tolliver uses the birdhouses, which are built by his son, as canvases on which he fashions arresting primitive paintings of birds and other animals; with their stark two-dimensionality, they recall the Paleolithic cave paintings of Lascaux and Altamira.

The Birdhouse as Art

In an age of increasing environmental awareness, birdhouses have themselves become the *subject* of art, as well as vehicles for a host of political, philosophical, and environmental viewpoints. In 1990, Wisconsin's Charles A. Wustum Museum of Fine Arts invited artists from all over to use the bird dwelling as an artistic point of departure, and the results ranged from the wry (Harriete Estel

Arts for the Birds created a birdhouse that truly deserves the name, top, and a fetching canine-faced coop, middle. At bottom, the inspiration for this vintage birdhouse of carved and painted wood must surely have been pure fantasy.

Two folk-art birdhouses from the American Primitive collection are designed in a "future Gothic" style unlikely to be seen in the realm of human architecture.

Berman's steel-and-wood houses "papered" with commercial cookie and cracker wrappers) to the unsettling (Jon Sontag's architectural Bird Mausoleum: Renaissance Model, with its life-size effigy of a deceased bird at the entry hole). Some of the houses in the exhibit appear fragile enough to decompose at any moment; others are menacing, barbed with spikes or thorns. They speak alternately of a supremely delicate environment and a terrifying threat to the natural world. Richard C. Newman's Bird Soul Catcher Monument is a totemic cross-shaped structure adorned with collaged images of skulls and masks, as frightening as it is beautiful.

No other contemporary artist has so thoroughly explored the

birdhouse theme as Laura Foreman. Her obsession with birdhouses began innocently enough, as she sat one afternoon in a vest-pocket park in the New York City neighborhood of TriBeCa. Like so many other neighborhoods in the city, TriBeCa, with its low rents and spacious warehouses, had once attracted artists, but as it gradually succumbed to gentrification, the artists were forced out. Looking around at the small patch of green, Foreman wondered if the birds, too, would soon find themselves homeless. It was then that she hatched an idea to design a series of birdhouses for the park, dedicated to the artists who had moved on. Alas, she was unable to find funding for the project, but it helped spark a new artistic direction. She has since created five site-specific birdhouses for New York City parks, including a Funky Birdhouse for the low-rent Lower East Side. Cobbled together with bits and pieces of demolition flotsam, it offers shelter to city-dwelling sparrows.

Her passion is clearly shared by scores of birdhouse builders, past and present, who have found in the form a unique expression of that ineffable quality we call the human imagination. Some have been motivated by humor, others by a sense of appreciation for nature, and still others by the need to express an opinion. Together, they have helped to lift birdhouse architecture out of the realm of the functional and elevate it to something as wondrous as the winged creatures who inhabit their creations.

Fanciful birdhouses can be streamlined and modern or appealingly kitschy. From Arts for the Birds, a wild green columnar house and a cuckoo clock for wrens, top, are more at home indoors than out. Bottom, Laura Foreman scavenged demolition sites for the components of her Funky Birdhouse, which now graces a New York City park.

5

....

COLLECTING AND DISPLAYING

You're at a flea market, or browsing the aisles of a rural antiques shop, and you spot it: a weathered old birdhouse that instantly brings to mind childhood summers in the country, the surprise of a blue robin's egg, languid afternoons filled with the scent of honeysuckle and the sound of birdsong. It's at that moment that you become a collector, forever under the spell of houses with thumbnail-size windows and barns no bigger than a bread box. Suddenly, you find

A striking architectural birdhouse—complete with dormer windows and portal—offers pleasant contrast to the formal neoclassic mirror above it.

yourself entranced by peeling paint and crumbling clapboard, and your heart quickens at the sight of bird scratches and swallow droppings. You can take comfort, of course, in the knowledge that you're not alone in your mania for these microdwellings. Birdhouses are increasingly valued as collectibles and one-of-a-kind examples of folk art.

Unfortunately—and inevitably—as demand has grown, so have prices. Though old birdhouses can still be found for reasonable amounts, many sell at exorbitant prices, with extraordinary examples sometimes carrying four-figure price tags. And the booming market for old birdhouses has spawned a host of reproductions, many of them crafted of recycled materials, and carefully "weathered" to take on the look of age. More than ever, then, the successful collector needs to know where to look, what to look for, and how much to pay for it.

Determining Value

New and reproduction birdhouses can be found almost everywhere, from chic housewares boutiques to department store chains to mail order catalogues. If authenticity isn't a priority, there's no reason to turn your nose up at these new, and often reasonably priced, houses—especially if you intend to use them out-of-doors. In addition, a host of talented craftspeople are carrying on the birdhouse tradition; though their creations may not see an immediate or exponential increase in value, these collectibles in their own right could very well appreciate over the years. The birdhouses of designers such as Randy Sewell, Michael Ridel, and Clifton Monteith are small pieces of contemporary art, and like the older birdhouses that inspired them, many are one of a kind.

The best way to recognize a stand-out birdhouse, new or old, is to familiarize yourself with what's out there. Steven Shapiro, whose Newmarket, Maryland, antiques shop specializes in birdhouses and other folk-art collectibles, advises collectors to look for unusual houses or those exhibiting a high degree of craftsmanship; no matter how old, he warns, common examples are going to remain common. Especially valuable are handmade touches: porches, pillars, chimneys, weathervanes, painted shrubbery, movable parts, houses embedded with buttons or bits of colored glass. Rather than detracting from a piece's value, weathering—chipped or worn paint, rusted nails, wood that's been gently warped by time and the elements—and evidence of use enhance collectibility. According to Susie Fisk-Stern, whose Ridgefield, Connecticut, shop sells old and new birdhouses, the most popular models are architectural and highly detailed. Geography, too, seems to play a part in determining collectibility. California dealer Judy Heidemann found that her customers preferred birdhouses with a traditional, countrified feeling—barns, cottages, peaked-roof bungalows. She suspects this represents a reaction to the predominant "cookie-cutter, tract-style" architecture of the area.

House Hunting

If you're looking exclusively for old birdhouses, the best buys can still be found at flea markets and farm sales, though more and more of these "finds" are being snapped up by dealers, often to be sold at many times their original prices. If you're determined to bypass the dealers, stick to rural areas of the United States, particularly in the South, Midwest, and New England, where most of the birdhouses were originally made and used. On the other hand, a reputable dealer—someone you know and trust—can steer you away from

A Biedermeier-style birdhouse would surely please discerning songbirds, but seems most comfortable in an elegant interior.

slick reproductions, and will often help you to locate specific styles and vintages.

Most older birdhouses on the market date from this century, though a few late-nineteenth-century models can still be found. Because they were usually crafted of perishable materials, and were used almost exclusively out-of-doors, birdhouses tended to succumb to the ravages of time and the weather (not to mention the birds and occasional rodents who made them their home). The majority of birdhouses that *did* manage to survive date from about 1910 through the 1940s.

Dating a birdhouse is no easy task, even for professionals. Prevailing architectural styles often offer a clue, though Victorian birdhouses, for example, have been popular from the 1900s to the present day. Embellishments can also help, especially datable ornaments like bottle caps and buttons. More important than pinning down an exact date is determining whether the birdhouse is genuinely old or a clever reproduction.

Because contemporary designers often use old barn wood in their birdhouses, Aarne Anton of New York's American Primitive Gallery always looks at the *edges* of the wood: newly cut edges will reveal tool marks and burrs. In many cases, these edges will be hidden or hand-softened to look old; if so, Anton advises, look at the entrance hole. Rain, sun, and the comings and goings of generations of birds tend to soften the edges of the entryway, and pecking and gnawing (by squatter rodents) often change its shape.

If the house is painted, look for a *gradation* in the weathering; the paint should be darkest under the eaves. Because they were frequently repainted, older houses tend to show layers of paint, often in a variety of colors. Hardware, too, can help unmask a pretender:

Folksy, funky, or elegantly architectural, birdhouses add visual interest to every conceivable interior style and can act as one-of-a-kind focal points.

look not just for rusted nails and screws (which can be easily faked) but vintage hardware *styles* (your local library can help here). And because older birdhouses were repaired from one season to the next, expect to find several *different* styles of hardware.

Finally, look for signs of use. Many older birdhouses still contain nests (sometimes layers of nests, if the houses couldn't be opened for cleaning). Bits of straw wedged into the woodwork and calcified droppings also indicate avian habitation. Beware the "antique" birdhouse with a spic-and-span interior.

Inside or Out?

Birdhouses were clearly designed for outdoor use, but not all can tolerate the out-of-doors. Most older birdhouses have endured decades of exposure to the elements; give them much more, and they're in danger of crumbling to dust. Even new birdhouses aren't necessarily weatherproof. Clifton Monteith's elegant and delicate bent-willow creations, for example, usually perch atop coffee tables and armoires; after years of outdoor use, he says, the natural-wood houses will begin to deteriorate. Find out from the manufacturer or craftsperson whether the house can tolerate outdoor exposure. If your interest in a birdhouse, old or new, is purely aesthetic—and if you've paid dearly for it—keep it inside. Hundreds of attractive contemporary birdhouses are designed to withstand the ravages of wind, sun, rain, and birds; stick to these if you're looking for a working birdhouse or garden ornament.

Nevertheless, some brave collectors insist on using their bird-

The sparse furnishings in this tower bedchamber highlight the room's spectacular proportions. A slender white birdhouse in the form of a country church enhances the serenity of the space and draws the eye to the elevated ceiling.

houses in the element for which they were designed. Alice Hoffman decorates her country house, inside *and* out, with the birdhouses she has collected over the years. She loves to cluster them in her garden, among the brilliance of summer flowers, and she keeps an oversized martin house on her back steps, where it can be easily admired from a living room window. Still, the rarest—and most expensive—houses in Hoffman's collection are snugly sheltered indoors.

One way to safely display a delicate birdhouse out-of-doors is to use it on a covered porch or in a screened sunroom. Susie Fisk-Stern shows off a tumbledown lighthouse/birdhouse on her Victorian porch; protected from the weather, it nevertheless seems very much in its element. On an eighteenth-century porch in Chesapeake, Virginia, a pillared birdhouse atop a nineteenth-century work table is part of a rural tableau, along with a chopping-block-turned-plant-stand, an antique dough-bowl, and an old wooden rake. The verandah of an Oregon farmhouse is decorated with flowers, quilts, and twig furniture; an old log birdhouse rests on a twig table alongside the nests that once decorated its interior. (Take note, however, that all birds, as well as their eggs and nests, are protected by the federal government; never remove a nest from the wild, and don't remove one from a birdhouse until you're sure the birds have left for the season.)

Porch and patio birdhouses need not be rustic to look at home in the out-of-doors. Against the porch wall of a whitewashed Colonial is a white church-style birdhouse from Lady Slipper Designs; it looks for all the world as if it were built into the original clapboard. And southwestern-style birdhouses of tin and painted wood adorn the adobe walls of many an enclosed Arizona patio.

Folk-art birdhouses have a natural affinity for country furnishings, as in this pine-paneled New England sitting room.

Decorating with Birdhouses

Part of the decorative appeal of birdhouses is their easy evocation of the out-of-doors. Hanging against lattice in a garden room or grouped with potted blooms on a wirework planter, birdhouses effectively bring an element of the outdoors to spaces that might otherwise seem enclosed. In the whimsically decorated potting shed of *Country Living* editor Niña Williams, a quintet of old birdhouses mingle on the open shelves of a painted armoire with terra-cotta pots, well-used gardening implements, and the muted pastels of dried flowers and herbs.

Of course, birdhouses make an eye-catching display in virtually any room of the house, equally at home on coffee tables, bedstands, and kitchen cabinets. In the dining room, a single architectural birdhouse, grouped with pots of flowering bulbs, makes a wonderful centerpiece for a Sunday brunch. Julie Stapleton, an Oregon antiques dealer, decorator, and birdhouse collector, groups birdhouses, nests, and sculptural moss-entwined branches for an outdoor effect in a corner of her dining room. (She sells her own painted birdhouses at her Estacada shop, the Tole Barn.)

Birdhouses have an affinity for natural materials; in a California beach house, a small blue-painted birdhouse is the stand-out element in a striking arrangement of driftwood, dried mesquite, and tumbleweed. And against the exposed-brick walls of the New York City floral shop VSF, a lean-to birdhouse looks right at home among dried hydrangeas, rosebuds, and gleaming pomegranates.

A single birdhouse—especially an elaborate or oversize model—can easily become the centerpiece of a room. But as any collector can attest, it's virtually impossible to resist the urge to add another—and another. Like the birds they were meant to shelter, birdhouses just seem to want to flock together.

BIRDHOUSE SPECIFICATIONS

Species	Diameter of Entry Hole (in inches)	Dimensions (in inches)	Entrance Above Floor (in inches)	Height Above Ground (in feet)
Bluebird species	1½	5 × 5 × 8	6	4–7
Chickadee species	1⅛	4 × 4 × 8	6–8	6–10
Common Flicker	2½	7 × 7 × 16–18	14–16	6–20
Hairy Woodpecker	1½	6 × 6 × 12–15	9–12	12–20
Downy Woodpecker	1¼	4 × 4 × 8–10	6–8	6–20
Red-bellied Woodpecker	2	6 × 6 × 12–15	9–12	12–20
American Kestrel	3	8 × 8 × 12–15	9–12	10–30
Screech-Owl species	3	8 × 8 × 12–15	9–12	10–30
Bewick's Wren	1–1¼	4 × 4 × 8	1–6	6–10
House Wren	1	4 × 4 × 8	1–6	6–10
Purple Martin	2	6 × 6 × 6	1	6–20
Tree Swallow	1½	5 × 5 × 6	1–5	6–15
Violet-green Swallow	1½	5 × 5 × 6	1–5	6–15
Tufted Titmouse	1¼	4 × 4 × 8	6–8	6–10
Wood Duck	4	10 × 10 × 25	18–20	12–40 or 2–5 over water

Nesting Shelves

Species	Dimensions (in inches)	Height Above Ground (in feet)
Barn Swallow	Base: 6 × 6	6–15
Eastern Phoebe	Height of Back: 8	
Say's Phoebe		
American Robin		

2" DIAMETER HOLE

Blueprint for a Purple Martin Gourd Condominium

MATERIALS

Obtain a minimum of 6 dried gooseneck-shaped gourds (gourds harvested in autumn and stored in a cool place over the winter are ready to use in early spring); polyurethane (optional); 1 wooden martin pole, at least 20′ high; and 2 to 3 pairs of wooden cross-pieces, about 3 feet long; heavy wire.

INSTRUCTIONS

Drill a 2″-diameter hole in the side of the gourd. This is the entryway for the birds.

Remove seeds and fibers from interior of the gourd. Drill 2 holes in the upper neck of the gourd; these are used for attaching the gourd to the crosspiece.

If you wish for the gourds to last longer than a single season, give them 2 coats of polyurethane; this will prolong their life to 2 years.

Nail crosspieces to martin pole where desired; wire or nail gourds to crosspieces at evenly spaced intervals. Erect martin pole by sinking it several feet into the ground to ensure its stability.

Blueprint for a Wren House

1A
30°
½"
1⅛" DIAMETER
HOLE IN FRONT

1B
6"
¼" VENTS IN BACK
9"
5"

4B
4A
1B
3B
3A
1A
2

2
1¾"   3"   1¾"
1¼"
6½"
4"
1¼"
6½"

3A+3B
4"
26°
7⅝"

4A+4B
7"
30°
5"

MATERIALS

Use cedar, pine, or fir of 1″ thickness, cut to the following dimensions: Two 6″ × 9″ boards (1A and 1B); one 6½″ × 6¼″ board (2); two 4″ × 7⅝″ boards (3A and 3B); two 5″ × 7″ boards (4A and 4B); two ¾″ × 4″ cleats.

INSTRUCTIONS

Bevel one 4″ edge of sides 3A and 3B at a 26° angle, and one 7″ edge of sides 4A and 4B at a 30° angle. Further, cut the top edges of sides 1A and 1B at a 30° angle to the horizontal. These will serve as the front and back of the birdhouse.

Make the entry hole for the front (side 1A) by drilling a circle at least 1⅛″ in diameter, but not much larger. This hole should be about 3″ from the top peak. Drill 5 evenly spaced ¼″-diameter vent holes along the top edges of side 1B.

Attach the cleats to the base (side 2) as illustrated, sides 3A and 3B at their unbevelled end to the cleats, and sides 1A and 1B to the ends of the cleats. The top, sides 4A and 4B, should be attached last, with their bevelled edges fitting snugly together.

Blueprint for a Bluebird House

1A — 1½" HOLE — 8" — 6" — 7"

1B — 11" — 3" — 7"

3A + 3B — 3" — 30° — 8" — 5"

2 — 5" — 5"

4 — HINGES — 7½" — 7"

MATERIALS

Use cedar, pine, or fir of 1″ thickness, cut to the following dimensions: One 7″ × 8″ board (1A); one 7″ × 11″ board (1B); one 5″ × 5″ board (2); two 5″ × 11″ boards (3A and 3B); one 7″ × 7½″ (4); 2 hinges.

INSTRUCTIONS

Cut the corners off the 5″-square board, which will serve as the base (side 2), to provide 4 drainage holes.

Drill a hole 1½″ in diameter on side 1A, 6″ from the bottom. This will serve as the front of the birdhouse.

Cut the top of the two 5″ × 11″ boards (sides 3A and 3B) at a 30° angle, 3″ from the top of the board, and drill 3 evenly spaced ¼″-diameter vent holes along the top edge of each board.

Attach the front and sides to the base, and nail the assembled sides to the back of the birdhouse (side 1B) 3″ from the bottom. Fasten the top (side 4) to the back with 2 hinges, and nail the house, facing away from the prevailing winds, to a post or tree.

SOURCES

Craftspeople/Designers

Cary and Janice Bills
Route 5, Box 78
Lewisburg, TN 37091
(615) 276-2306
Architectural birdhouses with a
"vintage" look.

Mary Donald Inc.
457 Schoolhouse Lane
Devon, PA 19333
(215) 293-1441
Decoratively painted
birdhouses.

Laura Foreman
(212) 227-9067
One-of-a-kind, highly
original birdhouses.

Garden Source Furnishings
200 Bennet Street
Atlanta, GA 30309
(404) 351-6446
Folk-art-inspired architectural
birdhouses.

Larry Kenosha
Bright Development Services
1010 West Brook Way
Hopkins, MN 55343
(612) 938-6178
Log cabin-style birdhouse
crafted of Minnesota materials.

Barry Leader
Arts for the Birds
122 West High Street
Elizabethtown, PA 17022
(717) 367-2990
Whimsical painted-wood
birdhouses.

Clifton Monteith
P.O. Box 9
Lake Ann, MI 49650
(616) 275-6560
Elegant hand-crafted wood and
bent-twig birdhouses.

Randy Ouzts
P.O. Box 261
Belmont, NC 28012
(704) 825-3046
Birdhouses and feeders crafted
from wood, kudzu, and other
vines.

Michael Ridel
The Wood Shed
12169 Greenock Lane
Los Angeles, CA 90049·
(213) 658-4519
Detailed architectural
birdhouses.

Randy Sewell
38 Muscogee Avenue N.W.
Atlanta, GA 30305
(404) 239-9130
Painted-wood architectural
birdhouses inspired by vintage
American roadside architecture.

The Streck Family
805 D Early Street
Santa Fe, NM 87501
(505) 984-8265
Southwestern-style painted-
wood birdhouses with tin and
copper details.

Nancy Thomas Studio Gallery
P.O. Box 274
Yorktown, VA
Decoratively painted
birdhouses.

Manufacturers/Distributors

*The making of birdhouses is, in gen-
eral, a cottage industry, and the
distinction between craftspeople and
manufacturers is often slight. Many of
the firms listed below employ or are
owned by talented artisans, and most
of their birdhouses are hand-crafted.*

Added Oomph
P.O. Box 6135
High Point, NC 27262
(919) 886-4410
Spectacular fiberglass birdhouse
in the shape of a garden folly.

Back Shore Woodworks
P.O. Box 33
Chamberlain, ME 04541
(207) 677-3625
Decorative, bird-friendly
birdhouses and feeders.

Bird Buddies
4005 Crawford Road
Spicewood, TX 78669
(800) 621-8407
Decorative rustic-style
birdhouses and feeders.

Country Originals
3844 West Northside Drive
Jackson, MS 39209
(601) 366-4229
Fanciful wood and tin
birdhouses; bee skep birdhouse.

English Thatch
P.O. Box 130287
Houston, TX 77219
(713) 524-7415
Thatched-roof birdhouses

Lady Slipper Designs
Route 3, Box 556
Bemidji, MN 56601
White painted-wood birdhouses
in a variety of architectural
styles. Write for list of retailers.

Lazy Hill Farms
P.O. Box 235
Colerain, NC 27924
(919) 356-2828
Cedar and cypress birdhouses
and feeders in traditional styles,
including shingle-roofed
English dovecotes.

Milano Series
(914) 699-3050
Modern and Postmodern
architectural birdhouses.

Remington Freeman Ltd.
225 Fifth Avenue
New York, NY 10010
(212) 689-5542
Distributors of a variety of
rustic and other birdhouses.

Terra Cotta Creations
Route 2, Box 160
Nixa, MO 65714
(417) 725-1108
Terra-cotta birdhouses.

Retailers

Because of their popularity and collectibility, birdhouses can be found in an increasing number of shops and galleries—even department stores. The list below is by its nature selective. Don't hesitate to investigate retailers in your area, particularly home-design emporia, country stores, and garden-furnishings shops.

ABC Carpet & Home
888 Broadway
New York, NY 10003
(212) 473-3000
Birdhouses in a variety of styles.

American Primitive Gallery
596 Broadway, Suite 205
New York, NY 10012
(212) 966-1530
Extensive selection of vintage
and new folk-art birdhouses.

Birdnest of Ridgefield
2 Big Shop Lane
Ridgefield, CT 06877
(203) 431-9889
Anything related to wild
birding, including new and
vintage birdhouses.

Birdwatchers General Store
36 Route 6A
Orleans, MA 02653
(508) 255-6974
Wide selection of bird-friendly
houses and feeders.

Cherishables
1608 20th Street N.W.
Washington, DC 20009
(202) 785-3616
Miniature birdhouse ornaments.

Crow's Nest Birding Shop
Cornell Laboratory of
Ornithology
159 Sapsucker Woods Road
Ithaca, NY 14850
(607) 254-2400

Nesting boxes and shelves,
finished or in kit form.

Dovetails
511 East Water Street
Charlottesville, VA 22901
(804) 979-9955
Vintage birdhouses.

Flights of Fancy
450 East 78th Street
New York, NY 10021
(212) 772-1302
Decorative rustic birdhouses
and feeders.

Growingthings
81-A Seventh Avenue
Brooklyn, NY 11217
(718) 638-0918
Wildly ornamented rustic-style
birdhouses.

Lexington Gardens
1008 Lexington Avenue
New York, NY 10021
(212) 861-4390
Decorative birdhouses.

Massachusetts Audubon Shop
South Great Road
Lincoln, MA 01773
(617) 259-9661
Houses, kits, and nesting
shelves for eleven species.

The Sampler
96 Summit Avenue
Summit, NJ 07901
(908) 277-4747
Wide selection of decorative
birdhouses, and a display of
vintage birdhouses.

Shapiro and Stambaugh
Eighth Alley
Newmarket, MD 21774
(301) 865-5027
Interesting selection of vintage
birdhouses.

Wild Goose Chase
1631 Sunflower Avenue
Santa Ana, CA 92704
(714) 966-2722
Good selection of vintage folk-
art birdhouses. (See their next-
door shop, Sweet William, for
newer houses.)

Zona
97 Greene Street
New York, NY 10021
(212) 925-6750
Unusual rustic-style birdhouses.

Catalogues/Mail Order

*A growing number of catalogues offer
birdhouses and feeders by mail, but
because their merchandise varies from
season to season, they have not been
included here. The catalogues listed
below are distinguished by their
unique selections.*

Kinsman Company, Inc.
River Road
Point Pleasant, PA 18950
(215) 297-5613
(800) 733-5613
German "wood-crete" bird-
houses, open swallow boxes.

Plow & Hearth
301 Madison Road
Orange, VA 22960
(800) 627-1712
Bluebird, wren, and bat houses,
robin shelves, swallow nesting
dishes, and predator guards.

Winterthur Gift & Garden
Sampler
Winterthur Museum and
Gardens
Dover, DE 19901
(800) 767-0500
Decorative wood and terra-cotta
birdhouses, including replicas of
the bluebird houses found in the
gardens at Winterthur.

Organizations

*In addition to the organizations listed
below, local Audubon Society chap-*

*ters can provide information on bird-
houses and bird housing.*

Bat Conservation International
P.O. Box 162603
Austin, TX 78716
This nonprofit organization is
dedicated to reversing the severe
decline in bat populations.

National Wildlife Federation
1400 16th Street, N.W.
Washington, DC 20036
The federation's Backyard
Wildlife Habitat Program shows
homeowners how to attract
birds and other wildlife by
providing food and cover.

North American Bluebird
Society
P.O. Box 6295
Silver Spring, MD 20916
The society has been responsible
for helping to preserve
America's precious and
threatened bluebirds. Write for
information on bluebird
preservation or to order houses
for eastern and western
bluebirds.

BIBLIOGRAPHY

Buff, Sheila. *The Birder's Catalogue*. New York: Simon & Schuster, 1989.

Cosgrove, Irene. *My Recipes Are for the Birds*. New York: Doubleday, 1976.

Davison, Verne E. *Attracting Birds*. New York: Thomas Y. Crowell, 1967.

DeGraaf, Richard M., and Gretchin M. Witman. *Trees, Shrubs, and Vines for Attracting Birds*. Amherst, MA: University of Massachusetts Press, 1979.

Dennis, John V. *A Complete Guide to Bird Feeding*. New York: Alfred A. Knopf, 1975.

Harrison, George H. *The Backyard Bird Watcher*. New York: Simon & Schuster, 1979.

Henderson, Carol L. *Woodworking for Wildlife*. St. Paul, MN: Minnesota Department of Natural Resources, 1984.

Kress, Stephen W. *The Audubon Society Guide to Attracting Birds*. New York: Charles Scribner's Sons, 1985.

———. *The Audubon Society Handbook for Birders*. New York: Charles Scribner's Sons, 1981.

McNeil, Don. *The Birdhouse Book*. Seattle: Pacific Search Press, 1979.

Schultz, Walter E. *How to Attract, House and Feed Birds*. New York: Macmillan, 1970.

Stokes, Donald and Lillian. *The Bird Feeder Book*. Boston: Little, Brown, 1988.

———. *The Complete Birdhouse Book*. Boston: Little, Brown, 1990.

Terres, John K. *Songbirds in Your Garden*. New York: Hawthorn Books, 1977.

Wade, J. L. *Attracting Purple Martins*. Griggsville, IL: Nature Society, 1987.

Weber, Dorothy Fitzcharles. *Artistry in Avian Abodes: The Little Birdhouse Book*. Williamsburg, VA: Williamsburg Publishing.

Wells, Malcolm. *Classic Architectural Birdhouses and Feeders*. Brewster, MA: 1989. (Because the book is self-published, it can most easily be obtained from the author, at 673 Satucket Road, Brewster, MA 02631).

PHOTO CREDITS

INDEX

. . . .

INDEX

· ·

86